7539

W9-AYD-748

ISAAC ASIMOV'S
Library of the Universe

The Asteroids

by Isaac Asimov

Gareth Stevens Publishing
Milwaukee

Library of Congress Cataloging-in-Publication Data

Asimov, Isaac, 1920-
   The asteroids.

   (Isaac Asimov's library of the universe)
   Bibliography: p.
   Includes index.
   Summary: Discusses the asteroids of our solar system and the possible
importance they might have for us in the future.
   1. Asteroids—Juvenile literature. [1. Asteroids] I. Title. II. Series: Asimov,
Isaac, 1920-   Library of the universe.
QB651.A84   1988   523.4'4   87-42598
ISBN 1-55532-378-2
ISBN 1-55532-353-7 (lib. bdg.)

A Gareth Stevens Children's Books edition. Edited, designed, and produced by

Gareth Stevens, Inc.
7317 West Green Tree Road   Milwaukee, Wisconsin 53223, USA

Text copyright © 1988 by Nightfall, Inc.
End matter copyright © 1988 by Gareth Stevens, Inc. and Martin Greenberg.
Format copyright © 1988 by Gareth Stevens, Inc.

First published in the United States and Canada by Gareth Stevens, Inc.

Cover painting © MariLynn Flynn

Designer: Laurie Shock.
Picture research: Kathy Keller.
Artwork commissioning: Kathy Keller and Laurie Shock.
Project editors: Mark Sachner and MaryLee Knowlton.

Technical adviser and consulting editor: Greg Walz-Chojnacki.

2 3 4 5 6 7 8 9 93 92 91 90 89 88

CONTENTS

Introduction 3
Rockpile of the Solar System 4
The Minor Planets 6
The Moons of Mars — A First Look at Asteroids? 8
All Shapes and Sizes 10
Jupiter's Army of Asteroids 12
Far-Out Asteroids 14
The Oddball Asteroids — Burnt-Out Comets? 16
Asteroids and Earth — Look Out Below! 18
Resources from Space 20
Visiting the Asteroids 22
Mining the Asteroids 24
New Outposts 26

Fact File 28
More Books About Asteroids 30
Places to Visit 30
For More Information About Asteroids 30
Glossary 31
Index 32

Introduction

We live in the Universe, an enormously large place. It's only in the last 50 years or so that we've found out how large it really is.

It's only natural that we would want to understand the place we live in. In the last 50 years we have developed instruments with which to get such understanding. We have radio telescopes, satellites, probes, and many other things that have told us far more about the Universe than could possibly have been imagined when I was young.

Nowadays, we have seen planets close up. We have learned about quasars and pulsars, about black holes and supernovas. We have learned amazing facts about how the Universe may have come into being and how it may end. Nothing can be more astonishing and more interesting.

Most of the objects in the Universe are huge — planets, suns, galaxies. But there are small objects, too. These would be too small to see if they were very far away from us, but some of them are right here, in our own Solar system. Just beyond the planet Mars, there are thousands of small bodies called asteroids.

They come in a grand variety of shapes and sizes. Some come very close to us at times, and some are quite far away. Some go about the Sun in peculiar paths. In this book we will talk about these asteroids and how important they may be to us some day.

In this artist's rendition of the asteroids, our view is from just beyond Jupiter. Also clearly visible are Mars, which is just within the belt of asteroids, and Earth. Near the Sun, which glows faintly from about 500 million miles (800 million km) away, Venus and Mercury are just visible.

Rockpile of the Solar System

When is a planet not a planet? — When it's an asteroid.

Take Ceres (pronounced "series") for example! In 1801, a new planet, smaller than any other, was discovered between the orbits of Mars and Jupiter. It was only about 600 miles (960 km) across, and it was named Ceres. In a few years, astronomers found still more planets in the same region, all of them even smaller than Ceres. They seemed like a pile of large rocks circling the Sun. We call them minor planets. We also call them asteroids, which means "star-like." They are so small that they seemed to be just dots of light that looked like stars, even through telescopes.

About 3,000 asteroids have been discovered, and there may be hundreds of thousands more.

© Andrew Chaikin

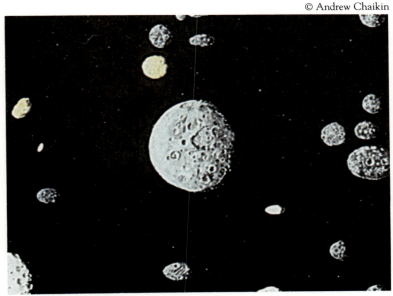

A portrait of Ceres, the major minor planet.

The Minor Planets

Actually, astronomers were looking for these asteroids, even though they may not have known it. Does this sound odd? Well, one astronomer had noticed that the planets in the Solar system seemed to be spaced in a regular pattern. But the space between Mars and Jupiter didn't fit the pattern. The large space between them led astronomers to expect another planet between them. The planet would have to be a small one, or else it would already have been seen. When Ceres was found, they thought, "Aha, there's the missing planet!" But the real surprise came when they found not one, but thousands of planets in the space between Mars and Jupiter! That space is called the asteroid belt.

Stumbling onto Ceres

A group of German astronomers planned to search the heavens for a possible planet between Mars and Jupiter. They carefully chose different sections of the sky among themselves, and made all the necessary arrangements. Then, just before they were ready to start, word came that an Italian astronomer, Giuseppe Piazzi, who wasn't looking for new planets at all, happened to stumble onto it while he was watching for other things. He discovered Ceres, on January 1, 1801.

Left and below: These illustrations clearly show the position of the asteroid belt between Jupiter and Mars. Also shown are the two clumps of asteroids that lead and trail Jupiter in its orbit around the Sun. These diagrams are not drawn to scale. The Sun, for instance, is actually more than 100 times greater than Earth in size.

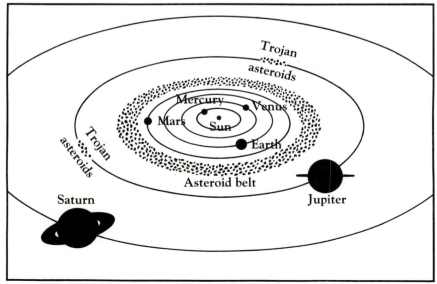

© Lynette Cook 1988

The Moons of Mars — A First Look at Asteroids?

Mars is just at the inner edge of the asteroid belt. Some asteroids might get trapped by Mars' gravity. In fact, Mars has two small moons that might be trapped asteroids. Mars' two moons, Phobos and Deimos, don't look like Mars at all. Mars is light in color, and reddish. The two moons are dark, as are many asteroids. Some rocket probes passing near Mars have taken close-up pictures of the two moons of Mars. These are probably the first good looks we have ever had of asteroids. Some day, rockets may land on the moons and study them even more closely.

A narrow portion of the asteroid belt stretches across this view of space. Closer to our vantage point are Mars and its two moons. Could tiny Deimos (left) and Phobos be asteroids yanked into orbit around Mars?

In search of the lost asteroid

When Ceres was discovered, it was too close to the Sun to be seen for long. Pretty soon, it couldn't be seen — and it hadn't been watched long enough for astronomers to work out its path. They feared it might not be found again! But there was a German mathematician, Karl Gauss, who was among the best mathematicians who ever lived. He figured out a new way of calculating planetary paths, worked one out for Ceres, and predicted exactly where it would be when it came out on the other side of the Sun. When the time came, astronomers looked — and there it was.

Hector: a single dumbbell-shaped asteroid or a pair of kissing cousins?
Very few asteroids are actually round, and Hector certainly proves the point!

All Shapes and Sizes

No asteroid has ever been discovered that is larger than Ceres, but there must be dozens that are more than 100 miles (160 km) across. Most asteroids, however, are only a few miles across and look more like flying mountains than planets. Some are dark like the moons of Mars, but some are very bright. One of the earliest discovered is Vesta, which reflects so much light it can sometimes just barely be seen even without a telescope. The small asteroids are brick-shaped or have other queer shapes. One, called Hector, is supposed to have a dumbbell shape. Perhaps it's really two asteroids melded into one. The truth is, only the largest asteroids actually look like round balls.

© Andrew Chaikin

A portrait of Vesta, one of the brightest asteroids in the sky. Only the fourth asteroid to be discovered — after Ceres, Pallas, and Juno — Vesta was first spotted and identified in 1807. It would be another 40 years before the discovery of any more asteroids.

Naming the asteroids — 1,000 and counting!

At first asteroids were named after goddesses such as Ceres, Pallas, Vesta, Juno, and so on. However, when great numbers were discovered, it became hard to think up names. They began to be named for astronomers, for other famous people, for girlfriends, for cities, for colleges, and so on. Since the names were supposed to be feminine, we have asteroids named Washingtonia and Rockefellia. The thousandth was named Piazzia after the man who discovered the first asteroid. One asteroid was named Drake, but to make it different, perhaps more feminine, it was spelled backward so the name is Ekard.

Jupiter's Army of Asteroids

Jupiter, the huge planet at the outer edge of the asteroid belt, has captured many asteroids. It has eight small moons circling it at large distances, and all of them are probably captured asteroids. There are also a number of asteroids that follow Jupiter in its orbit, and others that move ahead of it in its orbit. If you draw a line from Jupiter to each group of asteroids, and then draw lines from Jupiter and both groups to the Sun, you will have two equal-sided triangles. These groups are called Trojans because they were named for heroes in the ancient Greek tales of the Trojan War.

Jupiter and the Trojan asteroids in orbit around the Sun. As this diagram illustrates, even in their trek around the Sun, Jupiter and its army of asteroids hold to their steady formation.

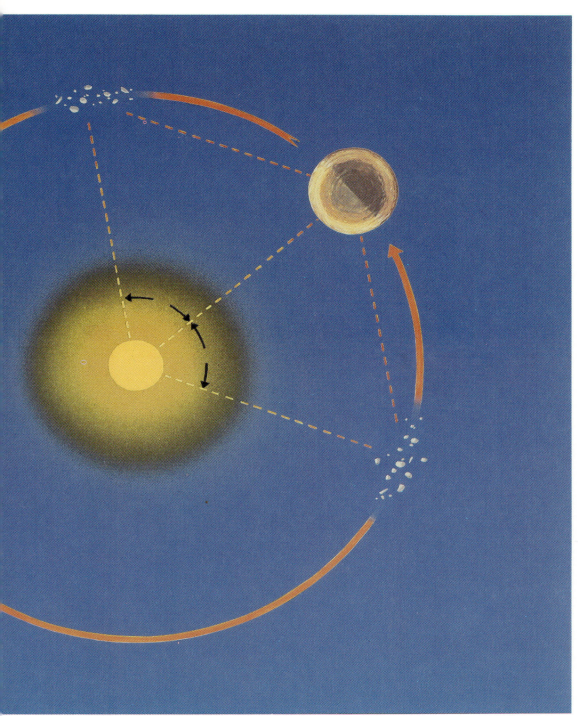

13

Far-Out Asteroids

A few asteroids lie far out beyond the asteroid belt — beyond even Jupiter and its faithful family of asteroids. The asteroid Hidalgo swoops out nearly to Saturn, and another, Chiron, moves in the space between Saturn and Uranus. Astronomers think Saturn's outermost moon, Phoebe, may be a captured asteroid. And Neptune's outer moon, Nereid, may be one, too. There are even astronomers who think that the farthest planet, Pluto, and its moon, Charon, are so small that they should be considered asteroids, too. There may be many asteroids in the outer reaches of the Solar system. But they are so distant that only the very largest are seen.

© David Hardy

Appearances can be deceiving! Tiny Hidalgo seems to dwarf Jupiter as it approaches the red giant in the reaches of our Solar system beyond the asteroid belt.

14

© David Hardy

A portrait of Pluto and Charon. What is the real nature of their relationship — a planet and its satellite? a double planet? or a pair of revolving asteroids?

Sizing up Ceres — big asteroid or small planet?

When Ceres was first discovered, everyone was surprised at how small it was. It was only 600 miles (960 km) across, about the width of France, while Mercury, the smallest planet besides Pluto, was over 3,000 miles (4,800 km) across, about the width of North America. However, when the other asteroids were discovered, astronomers began to be surprised at how <u>big</u> Ceres was. It was twice as large across as any other asteroid. It had five times as much mass as any other asteroid. In fact, some astronomers calculate that Ceres has one-tenth as much mass as all the other asteroids put together. Why should it be so large? We don't know.

The Oddball Asteroids — Burnt-Out Comets?

So now we know that most asteroids are found between Mars and Jupiter, while others lie even farther out. But not all asteroids behave like ordinary asteroids. A few have long, thin orbits that take them much closer to the Sun. Such orbits resemble the orbits of some comets. Recently astronomers have carefully studied the light from some of these asteroids and have found that they look more like comets than asteroids. They suspect that many asteroids that come near the Sun aren't really asteroids at all. Instead, they may really be old comets that no longer glow like ordinary comets.

The shiniest asteroid — but why?

The brightest asteroid is Vesta. It is only about 300 miles (480 km) across. It is the third largest asteroid but only half the size of Ceres. But Vesta reflects so much more light than Ceres does that it is actually brighter than Ceres at times. In fact, if you know exactly where to look and have very sharp eyes, you can see Vesta without a telescope. Yet it was only the fourth asteroid to be discovered. We don't know why it is so shiny. It may be covered with ice, but why should it be covered with ice when Ceres isn't?

Its glow mostly gone, an old comet nucleus keeps its
appointment with the Sun.

Apollo, a scant 2 miles (3 km) in diameter, flirts with
Earth. Just about every asteroid that comes close to
Earth is quite small.

Asteroids and Earth — Look Out Below!

Some asteroids move quite close to the Sun. Dozens, perhaps
even hundreds, move past Earth; some even past Venus and
Mercury. A few come so close to the Earth that they are called
Earth-grazers. In 1937, a small asteroid passed within 200,000
miles (320,000 km) of the Earth. That is closer than the Moon!
And in 1972, an asteroid fragment entered the Earth's atmosphere
over Idaho. It slipped through the atmosphere and back into space.
That was lucky, for it was as big as a house. And if it had hit the
Earth, probably somewhere near Alberta, it would have done a
great deal of damage. Some asteroids actually do strike the Earth.
Usually only small ones do, and no great harm is done. However,
in Arizona, there is a crater 3/4 mile (1.2 km) across where an
asteroid struck perhaps 50,000 years ago. We also know that
craters on other planets were caused by crashing asteroids.

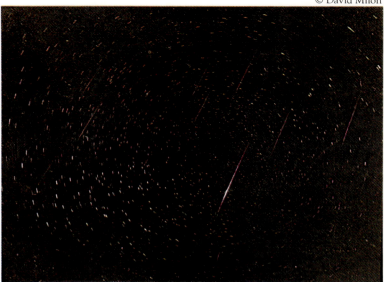

A photo of the Leonid meteor shower streaking across Earth's atmosphere. The Leonid showers occur every year, but they are exceptionally heavy every 33 years. The latest heavy occurrence was in 1966, so the next would be scheduled for 1999. Leonid meteors have actually been traced back to the year 902!

A remarkable event captured in a remarkable photo: Having entered Earth's atmosphere over Idaho, an asteroid — now a streaking meteor — flies above Jackson Lake, Wyoming. Astronomers believe it was 262 feet (80 m) in diameter, moved at an average speed of 33,000 miles (53,000 km) per hour, and weighed a million tons. It came within 36 miles (58 km) of the ground and traveled for 915 miles (1,473 km) before heading back into space.

Resources from Space

Asteroids that are just a few feet or meters across are called meteoroids. We see them as <u>meteors</u> when they enter Earth's atmosphere. If they strike (as meteor<u>ites</u>), they may even be useful. About one-tenth of the asteroids that strike Earth are almost pure nickel-iron. Thousands of years ago, before human beings learned how to get iron from ores, meteorites were the only supply of iron. They were valuable for making tools. Some day, when human beings are living on the Moon or in space, they might capture passing meteors for their metals.

Two views of humans working with asteroids, one past (below) and one future (above right). In the lower picture, a prehistoric man looking for iron examines a meteorite. In the upper picture, an astronaut works on an asteroid in space.

© David Hardy 1987

© David Hardy 1987

An astronaut draws samples from the surface of an asteroid. It may not be long before "fields" of asteroids become a rich natural resource for Earth.

© MariLynn Flynn 1983

Here is a view of an Earth-like Mars from a base on one of its moons.
Future technology might make it possible to terraform Mars — making
it Earth-like by putting new gases into its atmosphere, thereby trapping
sunlight and making its atmosphere like Earth's. Will Mars then
become our springboard to the asteroids and beyond?

© David Hardy

Visiting the Asteroids

Some day, after human beings have established a base on Mars,
they may venture outward farther still. With Mars as a base,
rocket probes may be sent to various asteroids. Perhaps even
astronauts will go out. Ceres is quite far from the Sun, and it
would be a very useful world on which to set up telescopes and
other instruments for studying the stars and the distant planets.
Studying asteroids themselves might tell us what they were made
of. That could give us some idea about the early days of the Solar
system and how the planets came to be.

A fanciful image of a miner taking samples from an asteroid. Note the movable arms on the craft, as well as the home ship in the background with yet another red exploration craft docked at its side.

Mining the Asteroids

Asteroids might become humanity's new mines in centuries to come. There must be tens of thousands that are lumps of iron. They could supply us with all the iron and steel we could ever want. Some are rocky and might serve as sources for other metals, and for oxygen, glass, concrete, and soil. Some are icy and might give us supplies of hydrogen, carbon, and nitrogen. These elements are not easy to come by outside Earth, and they are very necessary to human beings in space. Some asteroids might be hollowed out and made into space stations where people could live and work.

Mining diamonds from asteroids? It's quite possible, since asteroids contain carbon, the material from which diamonds are made. Here a team of miners examines its find as machines called mass drivers transport both mined materials and entire asteroids alike.

A team of asteroid explorers is greeted by a geyser. The matter shooting upward was once part of a comet that had slammed into this otherwise desolate asteroid.

© Mark Maxwell 1988   © Kurt Burmann 1988

The asteroids — a jigsaw planet?

Why are some asteroids made of iron, some of rock, and some of icy materials? If a planet like Earth broke up, pieces of its center would be iron, pieces of its surface would be icy, and pieces from in between would be rocky. Was there once a large planet between Mars and Jupiter that broke up? Maybe. But all the asteroids together would make up only a very small planet, and astronomers think it was too small to break up if it existed. So, maybe there wasn't a planet there after all. But why, then, the different kinds of asteroids? We don't know.

An assortment of machinery and craft at work in an asteroid-gathering mission. This artist's conception is based on an actual NASA study of the technology and planning that would be needed to put an asteroid into permanent orbit around Earth.

NASA

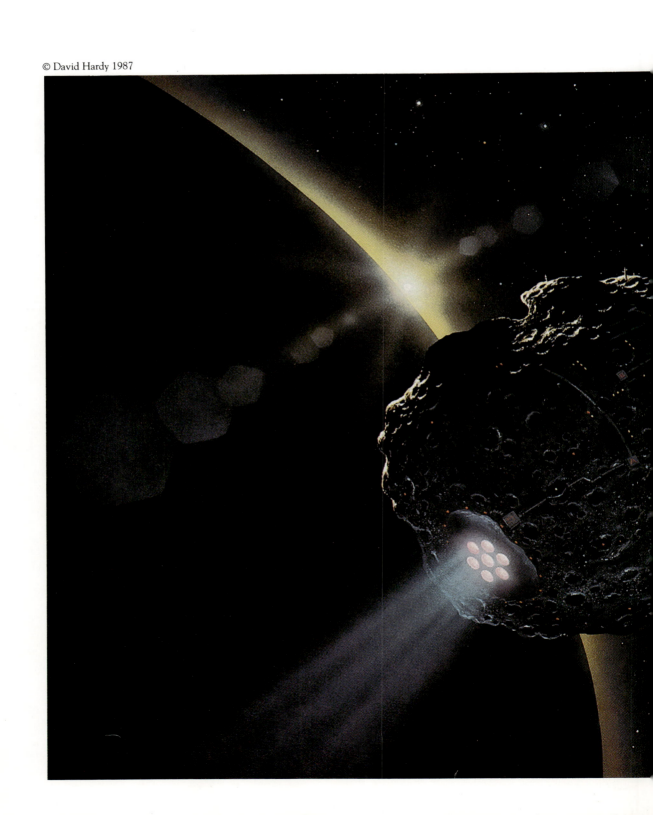

New Outposts

Once there are people living on the asteroids, these will serve as starting points for more exploration. People from the asteroids could build rockets to take them out to the moons of Jupiter and Saturn — and even farther. They might explore the entire Solar system. Perhaps some asteroids will be converted into huge starships and thousands of people on them will drift outward, away from the Sun forever, on a long, long journey to the distant stars. Who knows? The asteroids might play a role as human beings start to colonize the Galaxy — and begin their quest for other forms of intelligent life.

Science fiction or science fact? A hollowed-out asteroid, now a fully equipped spaceship, cruises past Jupiter on its way to the cosmos. Can you imagine people being born, growing up, raising families, and spending their entire lives as "space people" in ships like this? One day, it could happen.

Fact File: The Asteroids

There are thousands upon thousands of them, and they come in a variety of sizes and shapes. They look like bricks, dumbbells, mountains, cosmic sausages, and even the island of Manhattan! They are called names like Iris, Flora, Davida, Cincinnati, Marilyn, Russia, and Claudia. One is even called Photographica, in honor of photography — once the newest way of discovering them in space. Some, when discovered, are promptly "lost" from view. And one, Adalberta, was "discovered" — and then "undiscovered" because it never existed in the first place! We call them planetoids, minor planets, and occasionally, when they stray from their orbits, meteoroids. They are the asteroids.

Some "Firsts" and "Bests" of the Asteroids

Here are some offbeat "firsts" and "bests" of these offbeat members of our Solar system family — the asteroids. Keep in mind that new asteroids are being discovered all the time, and that records are made to be broken — even astronomical ones!

Record Set	Asteroid	Comments
Largest asteroid	CERES	Diameter: 623-646 miles (1,003-1,040 km)
Smallest known asteroid	HATHOR	Diameter: about 3/10 mile (0.5 km)
Brightest asteroid	VESTA	Only member of asteroid belt visible to naked eye
Darkest asteroid measured	ARETHUSA	Blacker than a blackboard
Shortest known rotation (spinning) period	ICARUS	2 hours, 16 minutes
Longest known rotation (spinning) period	GLAUKE	1,500 hours
First asteroid to be discovered	CERES	January 1, 1801
First asteroid to be discovered photographically	BRUCIA	December 20, 1891
Shortest time to revolve around Sun	RA-SHALOM	283 days (orbit is well within that of Earth)
Longest time to revolve around Sun	HIDALGO	Over 14 years (orbit is slightly beyond that of Saturn)**
First asteroid known to have a satellite	HERCULINA	Asteroid with diameter of 135 miles (217 km) was found to have a satellite with a diameter of 31 miles (50 km)
First masculine name for an asteroid	EROS	1898

** In 1977, an unusual object called Chiron was discovered. Its path is mostly between Saturn and Uranus, and it takes 50-68 years to orbit the Sun. For now, it has been designated as asteroidal, but it is no ordinary asteroid. Astronomers feel it may be a planetesimal (see Glossary) or even an escaped satellite of Saturn, and its statistics are not included in the record "bests" given on these pages.

The Biggest Babies of Our Solar System

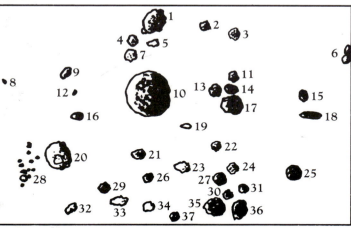

Here is an illustration, done to scale, of an assortment of asteroids — including all 33 known asteroids with diameters of 125 miles (200 km) or more. All asteroids are sized in proportion to one another and to the limb, or edge, of Mars on the left. The black-and-white drawing will guide you to the names of each asteroid, as well as to the Flora family of asteroids (Flores) with diameters greater than 9.5 miles (15 km).

			K E Y	
1 — Pallas	9 — Iris	17 — Hygiea	25 — Cybele	33 — Eunomia
2 — Winchester	10 — Ceres	18 — Camilla	26 — Thisbe	34 — Herculina
3 — Euphrosyne	11 — Bettina	19 — Dembowska	27 — Europa	35 — Interamnia
4 — Bamberga	12 — Nysa	20 — Vesta	28 — Flora/Flores	36 — Davida
5 — Daphne	13 — Patientia	21 — Eugenia	29 — Egeria	37 — Siegena
6 — Hector	14 — Themis	22 — Diotima	30 — Ursula	
7 — Juno	15 — Hermione	23 — Psyche	31 — Alauda	
8 — Eros	16 — Fortuna	24 — Loreley	32 — Hebe	

More Books About Asteroids

Here are more books about asteroids. If you are interested in them, check your library or bookstore.

Comets and Meteors. Asimov (Gareth Stevens)
Comets and Meteors. Couper (Franklin Watts)
Comets and Meteors. Fichter (Franklin Watts)
Our Solar System. Asimov (Gareth Stevens)
Sun, Moon and Planets. Myring (Usborne-Hayes)

Places to Visit

You can explore the asteroid belt and other places in the Universe without leaving Earth. Here are some museums and centers where you can find a variety of space exhibits.

Tour of the Universe
CN Tower
Toronto, Ontario

Science North
Sudbury, Ontario

NASA Lyndon B. Johnson Space Center
Houston, Texas

National Air and Space Museum
Smithsonian Institution
Washington, DC

NASA Lewis Research Center
Cleveland, Ohio

Kansas Cosmosphere and Space Center
Hutchinson, Kansas

For More Information About Asteroids

Here are some people you can write away to for more information about asteroids. Be sure to tell them exactly what you want to know about or see. And include your full name and address so they can write back to you.

For information about asteroids:
National Space Society
600 Maryland Avenue, SW
Washington, DC 20024

STARDATE
MacDonald Observatory
Austin, Texas 78712

About missions to the asteroids:
NASA Kennedy Space Center
Educational Services Office
Kennedy Space Center, Florida 32899

NASA Jet Propulsion Laboratory
Public Affairs 180-201
4800 Oak Grove Drive
Pasadena, California 91109

For catalogs of slides, posters, and other astronomy material:
AstroMedia Order Dept.
1027 N. 7th Street
Milwaukee, Wisconsin 53202

Hansen Planetarium
15 State Street
Salt Lake City, Utah 84111

Glossary

asteroid belt: the space between Mars and Jupiter that contains thousands of asteroids.

asteroid: "star-like." The asteroids are very small planets made of rock or metal. There are thousands of them in our Solar system, and they mainly orbit the Sun in large numbers between Mars and Jupiter. But some show up elsewhere in the Solar system — some as meteoroids and some possibly as "captured" moons of planets such as Mars.

Ceres: the first asteroid to be discovered (1801).

Chiron: an unusual asteroidal body whose path is usually between Saturn and Uranus. Astronomers think its diameter may be as large as 404 miles (650 km), but they aren't sure, and they think Chiron may be a huge planetesimal or even an escaped moon of Saturn.

Earth-grazers: asteroids that pass close to the Earth. Some of the smallest asteroids actually strike the Earth.

Gauss, Karl: a great German mathematician who calculated the paths of planets, including the path of the large asteroid Ceres.

galaxies: the numerous large groupings of stars, gas, and dust that exist in the Universe. Our Galaxy is known as the Milky Way.

Hector: an unusual asteroid that seems to be shaped like a dumbbell.

meteor: a meteoroid that has entered the Earth's atmosphere. Also, the bright streak of light made as the meteoroid enters or moves through the atmosphere.

meteorite: a meteoroid when it hits Earth.

meteoroid: a lump of rock or metal drifting through space. Meteoroids can be as big as asteroids or as small as specks of dust.

Piazzi, Giuseppe: the Italian astronomer who discovered Ceres, the first asteroid to be named.

planetesimals: small bits of matter that, when joined together, may have formed planets.

planetoid: another name for an asteroid. In a way, this is a more accurate name, since the asteroids, or minor planets, are more "planet-like" than they are "star-like."

Pluto: the farthest planet in our Solar system and one so small that some believe it to be a large asteroid.

Solar system: the Sun with the planets and all other bodies that orbit the Sun.

trapped asteroids: asteroids that are trapped by the gravity of planets. The moons of certain planets are in reality trapped asteroids.

Universe: everything that we know exists and that we believe may exist.

Vesta: the brightest asteroid. It has a diameter of about 300 miles (480 km).

Index

Alberta 18
Apollo 18
Arizona 18
Asteroid belt 4, 6-7, 8-9, 14

Ceres 5, 6-7, 9, 11, 15, 16, 22
Charon 14, 15
Chiron 14
Comets 16-17, 24

Deimos 8-9
Drake 11

Earth 4, 6-7, 18-19, 20, 21, 24-25
Earth-grazers 18
Ekard 11

France 15

Galaxy 27
Gauss, Karl 9
Gravity 8

Hector 10, 11
Hidalgo 14

Jackson Lake, Wyoming 19
Juno 11
Jupiter 4, 5, 6-7, 12-13, 14, 16, 25, 26-27

Leonid meteor showers 19

Mars 4, 5, 6-7, 8-9, 11, 16, 22, 25
Mercury 4, 15, 16, 18
Meteors, meteorites, and meteoroids 20
Mines and mining 20-21, 23, 24-25
Moon, Earth's 20
Moon, Pluto's 14, 15
Moons of Jupiter 12, 27

Moons of Mars 8-9, 11, 22
Moons of Neptune 14
Moons of Saturn 14, 27

Neptune 14
Nereid 14
North America 15

Pallas 11
Phobos 8-9
Phoebe 14
Piazzi, Giuseppe 7
Piazzia 11
Planets 5, 6-7, 9, 12, 14, 15, 18, 22, 25
Pluto 14, 15

Rockefellia 11
Rocket probes 8, 22

Saturn 14, 27
Solar system 4, 6, 14, 22, 27
Starships 26-27
Sun 4, 6-7, 9, 12-13, 16, 17, 18, 22, 27

Telescopes 5, 11, 16, 22
Trojans (asteroids) 12-13
Trojan War 12

Uranus 14
Utah 18-19

Venus 4, 18
Vesta 11, 16

Washingtonia 11
Wyoming 19

The publishers wish to thank the following for permission to reproduce copyright material: front cover, ©
MariLynn Flynn 1986; p. 21 (lower), © MariLynn Flynn 1983; pp. 4, 14, 15, 18, 20, 21 (upper) 22, 26-27, ©
David Hardy; pp. 5, 11, 29, © Andrew Chaikin; pp. 6-7 (both), © Lynette Cook 1988; pp. 8-9, © Kurt Burmann
1987; p. 24 (lower), © Kurt Burmann 1988; pp. 10, 17, © Julian Baum 1988; pp. 12-13, © Sally Bensusen
1988; p. 19 (upper), © Dennis Milon; p. 19 (lower), © James M. Baker; p. 23, © Lamar Savings, Austin,
Texas, by Pat Rawlings; p. 24 (upper), © Mark Maxwell 1988; p. 25, courtesy of NASA.